AN IDEAS INTO ACTION GUIDEBOOK

Giving Feedback to Subordinates

D1125116

IDEAS INTO ACTION GUIDEBOOKS

Aimed at managers and executives who are concerned with their own and others' development, each guidebook in this series gives specific advice on how to complete a developmental task or solve a leadership problem.

LEAD CONTRIBUTORS	Raoul J. Buron
	Dana McDonald-Mann
GUIDEBOOK ADVISORY GROUP	Victoria A. Guthrie
	Cynthia D. McCauley
	Russ S. Moxley
DIRECTOR OF PUBLICATIONS	Martin Wilcox
EDITOR	Peter Scisco
WRITER	Janet Fox
DESIGN AND LAYOUT	Joanne Ferguson
CONTRIBUTING ARTISTS	Laura J. Gibson
	Chris Wilson, 29 & Company
RIGHTS AND PERMISSIONS	Kelly Lombardino

CCL No. 403
ISBN-13: 978-1-882197-39-2
ISBN-10: 1-882197-39-9

CENTER FOR CREATIVE LEADERSHIP
WWW.CCL.ORG

AN IDEAS INTO ACTION GUIDEBOOK

Giving Feedback to Subordinates

Raoul J. Buron and Dana McDonald-Mann

Center for
Creative
Leadership®

This series of guidebooks draws on the practical knowledge that the Center for Creative Leadership (CCL) has generated since its inception in 1970. The purpose of the series is to provide leaders with specific advice on how to complete a developmental task or solve a leadership challenge. In doing that, the series carries out CCL's mission to advance the understanding, practice, and development of leadership for the benefit of society worldwide.

CCL's unique position as a research and education organization supports a community of accomplished scholars and educators in a community of shared knowledge. CCL's knowledge community holds certain principles in common, and its members work together to understand and generate practical responses to the ever-changing circumstances of leadership and organizational challenges.

In its interactions with a richly varied client population, in its research into the effect of leadership on organizational performance and sustainability, and in its deep insight into the workings of organizations, CCL creates new, sound ideas that leaders all over the world put into action every day. We believe you will find the Ideas Into Action Guidebooks an important addition to your leadership toolkit.

Table of Contents

IN BRIEF

If you're a manager with people who report directly to you, it's important that you give them feedback on their behavior and performance. Most of your employees want to do a good job. Many are unaware of the impact of their behavior on their job performance, for good or bad. Feedback from you, their manager, can help them identify what they are doing well and build on those skills, correct problems, and develop new abilities that improve not just their personal lives but also the organization in which they and you work. This guidebook will tell when you should give feedback, how you should deliver it, and how to manage its results.

Why Give Feedback to Subordinates?

Most of your employees want to do a good job. Many are unaware of the impact of their behavior on their job performance, for good or bad. Feedback from you, their manager, can help them identify what they are doing well and build on those skills, correct problems, and develop new abilities that improve not just their personal lives but also the organization in which they and you work.

Effective feedback provides the necessary information people need to build on their strengths and to shore up weaknesses. It's a powerful tool for accelerating learning and for developing mastery. Stop and think about the last time you learned a new skill. Whether it was golf or square dancing, you depended on the feedback from a professional or an experienced enthusiast to help you capitalize on your strengths and to see the weaknesses in your performance. Without such feedback, the probability is that you would not identify your best skills and that weaknesses and errors would become ingrained through practice and repetition.

Given its potential to bolster improved performance, managers should eagerly supply feedback to their subordinates. But it doesn't happen often. Most people work without the benefits of effective feedback. For whatever reason, managers find it hard to give the feedback to their subordinates that they need, want, and deserve.

To succeed in your leadership role, you must learn how to make feedback a part of developing your subordinates to their full potential. More than that, you must learn how to provide effective feedback that is empowering, not damaging; that is constructive, not debilitating. The purpose of this guidebook is to show you how and when to give effective feedback to subordinates.

When to Give Feedback to Subordinates

Giving feedback is not the same as holding an annual performance review. It's true that honest feedback is an essential ingredient in a formal review process, but the benefits of feedback occur as part of an ongoing process, not as a one-shot deal. Your goal is to create a relationship with your employees that allows you to give honest feedback about behavior and performance without putting them on the defensive. Timing is critical. You should give feedback regularly, give feedback at the moment it is needed, give feedback when development opportunities arise, and give feedback when it is necessary for an employee to modify behavior to improve performance.

Give Feedback Frequently

Because the benefits of feedback are accrued over time, you should give feedback often. This gives you the best chance of reinforcing positive behavior and of influencing change in unacceptable behavior. By frequently giving feedback, you will find it's easier to focus on a specific behavior. Giving frequent feedback also helps you develop a less formal approach to delivering your message. This kind of feedback need only take a minute.

> *Lucy, the logic of your argument in that meeting was very persuasive. You had my complete attention. I noticed that others were asking different kinds of questions at the end of your presentation than they were asking at the beginning. Your presentation moved me from skepticism to enthusiasm. Judging from the body language around the room, I think others shared that feeling.*

Make Feedback Timely

There's little value to dredging up a behavior that occurred six months earlier. Whether you want to reinforce or correct an employee's behavior, it's important to speak to the employee when the experience is fresh. If a subordinate's actions threaten the success of a task, now is the time to talk. You want to help your employee improve before another project derails.

> *Jake, you haven't kept your team informed of its progress on a timely basis. As a result, a project milestone was missed and I've had to move the completion date back two months. I am having doubts as to whether you can manage this team. Already, this delay will negatively impact product introduction and sales.*

Giving timely and frequent feedback lets you observe more of your subordinates' behavior. Too often, managers notice and comment only on extreme behavior—the truly outstanding performance or the truly dreadful gaffe. But almost everything an employee does falls between these extremes. Look for and give feedback on those more usual behaviors.

Offer Feedback for Development

Making employees aware of potential opportunities and providing constructive steps they can take to achieve those goals are key motivations for providing effective feedback to subordinates. Help your subordinates look to the future by guiding them to the action they need to take to succeed.

Let's take the case of Angela. You believe she would be a good person to manage the new branch office. She has most of the skills she needs to succeed there, and you can help her find resources so she can learn what she doesn't know. You want to let her know about this opportunity and to see if it fits in with her personal career goals.

> *Angela, your performance over the last several months, which we've talked about before, shows me that you've developed quite an array of skills. We're in need of a manager for the new branch office, and I think you would be the right choice for that position. Now, to be honest, there are a couple of areas that would be completely new to you. But the company has some excellent training opportunities that would help you build your skills, and we would make the time available to you to acquire that training. In addition, Bobbi Towers, who has managed our San Antonio branch since it opened two years ago, has agreed to be a mentor to whoever agrees to this assignment, and to help that person in whatever way is needed. Can you tell me if this kind of assignment fits in with your personal career plans?*

Use Feedback to Solve Performance Problems

If you are planning a feedback session to address a performance problem, don't deliver your feedback in the hall, off the cuff, or on the run. Your feedback session should be scheduled, private, focused, and structured. You know, perhaps from personal experience, how tense and unpleasant such feedback sessions can be. If you deliver regular and timely feedback on an ongoing basis, the relationship and trust you build with an employee can alleviate some of that pressure. But you must also think about what the employee's thoughts and reactions might be to your feedback. Timely and frequent feedback goes a very long way to creating an environment of trust in which you can deal with those reactions.

> *Larry is the kind of results-oriented manager that you value, but his style is abrasive to some. Now two of the people who report to him have resigned, both citing his abrupt, critical behavior as the reason.*

You have no doubt that this behavior is limiting his effectiveness as a manager. You do not know if he is aware of what he is doing to make his direct reports feel intimidated and inadequate. You do not know if he would be willing to modify his behavior. You have in mind a series of steps that could help him if he does want to work on that behavior. You tell him that you want to schedule a time to talk with him about a performance issue.

Your feedback might go something like this: Larry, two of your direct reports have resigned. Both of them said during their exit interviews that they were intimidated by your style of management. The fact that two people have left indicates to me that perhaps you're not aware of the impact that your behavior is having on your subordinates. I will say right now that we value your contributions to the company. I think you can contribute even more by passing on some of the passion you have for the job to the people under you. To do that, you need to appreciate the different ways in which people accept information and learn. If you're willing to accept that changes in your management style might achieve better results from your staff, the company is willing to send you through a leadership program to help you reach that goal.

When to Give Subordinates Feedback

Often

On Time

As an Opportunity for Development

To Solve a Performance Problem

How to Give Feedback to Subordinates

Creating, or seizing, an opportunity to give feedback to an employee is your first task. Next, you have to make your feedback effective. Compassionate and honest feedback from you will help your subordinates develop goals, make and reinforce positive changes, raise self-confidence, and spur action.

Be Specific

To increase the quality and effectiveness of the feedback you give, we recommend using the three-step process that we teach and practice at the Center for Creative Leadership: the Situation-Behavior-Impact model. Called SBI for short, this simple feedback structure keeps your comments relevant and focused to maximize their effectiveness. Essentially, SBI means you describe the **Situation** in which you observed the employee, you describe the **Behavior** you observed, and you describe the **Impact** of that behavior on you and others present in that situation.

> *Jim, I saw that presentation you made to the Excelsior group* **(Situation)**. *I liked how you picked up on their questions. I noticed that you were able to move out of your prepared presentation to address their concerns without missing a beat* **(Behavior)**. *They were all nodding their heads in agreement when you answered that question about the delivery time frame. You made me confident that you were in control of all the material and information. Joel Smythe told me afterwards that our company seems to have a much better understanding of Excelsior's situation than anyone else on their short list* **(Impact)**.

Feedback or Attaboy?

SBI feedback is not the same as a pat on the back. All of your subordinates would like to hear "You're doing a great job," or "We couldn't get along without you." Those "attaboys" might be great ego boosters but little else. The kind of feedback we support, practice, and teach informs your subordinates about what their strengths are, designates which of their skills are most valuable to the organization, and illustrates to them where you believe they have the ability to change and improve.

Do	Don't
Specify the situation. Describe a particular occasion, such as a specific staff meeting or a particular project.	Use phrases like "always" or "never" that put subordinates on the defensive.
Specify the behavior. Tell what you actually observed in the situation you have described.	Make general, vague characterizations ("You used bad judgment" or "You made a good presentation") that don't focus on behavior within a specific situation.
Specify the impact. Make it clear what impact your subordinate's specific behavior had on you and others.	Make exaggerated statements about the impact a behavior might have to the organization, or interpret the behavior's impact as the result of some other cause.

Keep It Simple

You may be accustomed to moving quickly to the impact or effect of a subordinate's behavior or action in order to get a solution. But if you want to encourage real development among your subordinates, slow down. Reduce your feedback to its essential elements. Recreate the situation in your mind and describe it. ("I'm glad you came to the staff meeting yesterday.") Describe the subordinate's behavior in that situation without embellishment. ("During the meeting you kept looking at your watch.") Make your comments as direct as possible, and stick to the impact that the behavior had on you. ("You made me feel like you didn't think our discussion was important.") Directness enforces honest feedback. Don't get ahead of yourself. Remember to go through each SBI step.

Keep Clear of Interpretations

In keeping your message simple, not only do you keep it direct and honest, but you limit it to the impact of the subordinate's behavior. If you observe troublesome behavior, you may be tempted to go beyond describing the impact to exploring reasons for the behavior. That invites misinterpretation that can damage the trusting relationship you've worked so hard to build. Even if you were perfectly correct in your attributions and interpretations, your subordinates are responsible for changing their behavior. You have to give them choices for making changes, not excuses for avoiding changes.

Don't Interpret . . .

Bill really turned that customer group off with his cold, arrogant manner. Of course he's going through an ugly divorce right now. But then he always was pretty distant and difficult. What else would you expect from somebody who grew up in a broken home?

Whoa! Attributing a specific behavior to some possible cause gets into dangerous territory. Think of the position you've just put Bill in. You just saw him turn off a customer group. Then you assumed that the behavior is because he's getting divorced. Then you leap to the conclusion that he can't help the way he acts because of the way he was raised. If you were to tell Bill all of this as feedback, what are the chances that he will change his behavior? What choices do you leave him? How responsible do you make him for the way he acted? Is there any reason for him to believe that you think he can do anything differently?

But Do Describe

Bill, I'd like to talk to you about our meeting this morning with the Grandmark team (S). You were really well prepared for that meeting and you had all the documentation with you, which was good. I noticed, though, that you cut Dan short two or three times when he was trying to get some information. You were paging through reports when Jean and Bob were trying to engage you in a dialogue (B). I was uncomfortable because they were not getting the information they were asking for. Long before the end of the meeting, the three of them were rolling their eyes and showing signs of exasperation. None of them responded to my suggestion that we get together again (I).

By confining feedback to the SBI structure, you avoid the assumptions and character assassinations that damage relationships and inhibit change. Feedback is not a personal attack. It's not a negative judgment on an employee's personality or morals. Appropriate feedback gives your subordinates room to grow.

How to Build the Feedback Relationship

In most organizations, annual reviews are the only institutionalized means of providing people with feedback on their performance. As you've learned, frequent feedback promotes a less formal approach and makes the entire process more comfortable for your subordinate and for you. That comfort in turn makes it possible for you to give honest and direct feedback that is specific, productive, and meaningful. A formal, annual performance review will not build the connection between you and your subordinate that is necessary for an effective session. For that, you need to build a feedback relationship.

Create Trust

The first step in building the feedback relationship is to catch people doing things right. Feedback succeeds best when you deliver it in a ratio of several positive comments for each negative one. This doesn't mean you should hold back your negative feedback and let the time slip away. We've already talked about how it's important to give feedback close to the time of the behavior. To create trust, you have to strike a balance between boosting an employee's confidence with feedback about a job well done and feedback about problematic behavior that needs to be addressed. When your subordinates understand that you are balanced in the way you give feedback, they will trust your comments as sincere and meaningful. They will trust your descriptions of the impact of their behavior on you and its implications to the organization.

Mary is an excellent brand manager and a dedicated, loyal employee. A creative thinker, she has good ideas and is adept at getting others to see the merit of adopting her ideas. She is a good team player, and generous in giving credit to other people for their contributions. But Mary talks too much. Her mind always seems to be racing, and she frequently interrupts, finishes people's sentences, and fails to draw out or listen to other points of view.

Leverage Strengths

Mary is like most of your subordinates. She is a good employee and you want to keep her. She has the potential to develop and to take on more responsibility, and to advance both her personal goals and the goals of your organization. One or two things are holding her back, and you are in a position to observe them and help her to change those behaviors if she so chooses.

Mary, you handled that customer complaint like a pro. You showed empathy and really calmed him down fast. You were really able to think on your feet and present him with some ingenious options for getting the problem solved . . .

First off, give Mary credit for everything she does right. It is through her strengths that she will be able to address her shortcomings. If you reinforce her confidence, she will be able to take the risk of looking at her weaknesses and trying to make changes. If you focus only on her weakness or problem behavior, Mary might feel angry that you've never noticed how much good she does for the organization. She might feel unappreciated for her good qualities and high contributions. Given that starting point, Mary isn't likely to feel motivated to change her behavior.

Balance Your Message

A feedback ratio of about 4:1 (positive to negative) creates the most favorable feedback climate, but be careful not to deliver all of that feedback in a "bad news sandwich." Let's return to Mary's situation.

> . . . but you kept interrupting him. That made me uncomfortable because I could sense that he wasn't too happy about being cut off. He could hardly get a word in edgewise once you got going. I really appreciate your quick mind and creative problem-solving, but be careful not to turn that strength into a weakness. Take time to listen carefully and fully to others' ideas.

You've given Mary at least four positive comments and one negative comment. On the surface, it appears that you're sticking with the 4:1 ratio. But you're working against yourself in delivering all of that feedback in a single session. Following the ratio of 4:1 doesn't mean you have to count up your positive feedback and negative feedback. You should look at how your positive and negative feedback balance over time. Any one feedback session may be positive or negative, but over a period of time you are building a ratio of positive-to-negative comments that enhances your professional relationship with your subordinate.

How to Structure the Feedback Session

Delivering honest, direct, effective feedback is difficult. Although many feedback situations can and should be handled informally, feedback about performance or development issues may require a more structured approach. As a leader, you can take steps to make these meetings more comfortable and productive.

1. Make an appointment in advance and let your subordinate know the purpose of the discussion. For example, you might say that since he or she has just taken on a special project, you'd like to discuss the development opportunities associated with that project. Or you might come to your subordinate just after he or she has completed a difficult project and say that you've noticed the struggles he or she had and you'd like to talk about some ways to address that problem. Your goal is to give your subordinate time to think about the upcoming session without causing undue worry or anxiety.

2. Give your subordinate a private setting and your undivided attention. Close the door. Don't take phone calls. You want to underline the fact that this is an important conversation. You want to give the employee a safe place in which he or she can listen, think, and respond to your feedback without interruptions or distractions.

3. Be sensitive to the imbalance of power. As the manager, the power is on your side. This is a time to deemphasize it. You might have your employee sit beside you rather than across

from you. Or you might consider having the discussion in some room other than your office, in a more neutral (but still private) setting.

4. Give your subordinate a chance to talk. After you've described the situation, behavior, and impact, ask for your employee's thoughts about what you have described. It's not at all uncommon for people to be unaware of the impact of their behavior. As often as not, you will hear a reaction of surprise. However your subordinate responds, even if it's a form of defensiveness, allow that response and accept it. You might ask if the individual has heard this kind of comment about him- or herself before, or noticed this kind of impact in other situations.

5. Offer suggestions and support for your subordinate's changing the behavior in the case of a performance problem, or for expanding skills in the case of professional development. Be ready to suggest constructive steps that your employee can take next.

How to Handle Feedback's Emotional Impact

By providing frequent, honest, and compassionate feedback, you're helping your subordinates grow and develop. You can't control how they feel about it, but you can and should use what you know about each employee to make your feedback the most constructive and beneficial it can be. You already know, from your management experience, that different people respond differently to information they receive about their performance. Understanding, anticipating, and mentally preparing yourself for the complexity of how your feedback will be received is part of the art of management.

Take Into Account the Individual Situation

Suzanne has worked for you for one month. She is clearly anxious about how well she is performing in this new job. You know she has the qualifications and experience, but she is coming across to colleagues and customers as hesitant and weak. You know that if she continues to withhold her ideas and avoid making decisions, she won't function well in her position.

You could give Suzanne feedback on the negative impact that her novice behavior is having, but that will probably only increase her anxiety. At this point, given your appraisal of the situation, you decide that Suzanne will benefit more from getting feedback on her positive behavior and assurances of your confidence in her.

Recognize That People Process Information Differently

You've just given Jeff feedback on the high number of errors his budget contains and the impact of all those mistakes. Jeff is very interested in doing well and getting ahead, and he's astonished by this information. He clearly had no idea that his work in this particular area was slipshod. But when you ask what specific actions he can take, Jeff offers only vague assertions and promises.

You could work out a plan for Jeff to begin assembling his reports earlier and to have his numbers checked by others before they are distributed. But you see that Jeff is surprised and chagrined, and you know that he would probably prefer to work out his own plan for correcting the problem. He needs time to absorb the bad news and to figure out what he needs to do differently. In giving feedback, you'll find that some subordinates understand your message instantly and move immediately into talking about all the implications and ramifications. Other subordinates need time and privacy to digest information, and hate to be put on the spot to make decisions on the basis of perceptions and suggestions that are brand new to them. If you press for a decision before such a person has had time to ponder, the result is likely to be a bad choice and a weak commitment. These differences are not defects or weaknesses but have strong implications for how people express themselves and how they react to new information and novel situations.

Factor in Health, Personal, and Family Problems

Michelle is one of your most promising subordinates, and now there is a great opportunity for her to develop her skills and advance her career. You would like to put her in charge of training in a particular system at your field locations around the country. This would involve her traveling two days a week. When you present this idea to her, Michelle bursts into tears.

When you give Michelle a chance to talk, you find out that she is in the process of moving her mother into a nursing home. This is a terribly difficult situation because the mother expected that Michelle would quit her job to care for her. Michelle has had her eye on that training and traveling opportunity, and by cruel fate, it seems to her, it has come along at the very time when she must devote extra time to her mother and can't even consider overnight trips. Stresses and problems outside of work contribute to how people perform at work. When you know about temporary difficulties, you can adjust the timing and content of your feedback accordingly. But you must be prepared to have unexpected information crop up in feedback situations.

Draw on Your Subordinate's Problem-solving Abilities

Marcus has brilliant analytic and technical skills. But putting him on the sales team has not worked out well. At meetings where he must present technical information to customer teams, he is losing sales. He bombards the customers with far more information than they want or need, and throws technical jargon around right and left. During those meetings, his actions strike you as arrogant and insensitive. He doesn't look you in the eye. You give Marcus this specific feedback, with the idea that he, like you, will conclude that he should be removed from the sales team, even though he volunteered for that assignment.

Marcus surprises you. He is very interested in sticking with this assignment and learning to get it right. Learning how to present technical information effectively to nontechnical people is high on his personal development agenda. He's also quite aware of the negative impact of his behavior, and he's already taking some steps to improve. He's working through a self-teaching book on presentation skills. He'd like to know if you can suggest other resources that would help him get up to speed quickly on these skills. People who are motivated to do well in their work often can work out their own solutions to problems you bring to their attention. In giving feedback, you should give them that opportunity before telling them how you propose to fix the problem. The solution the subordinate works out will not feel like a punishment, and may very well suit his or her personality and style better than any solution you could devise.

Practice Makes Permanent

Like the other leadership skills you have developed, giving feed-back to subordinates may at first feel unnatural and uncomfortable. Don't be concerned if your initial attempts are awkward. Take that first step. Give feedback often to build your confidence and to create a trusting relationship with your subordinates that you can use to provide honest feedback that delivers your message clearly.

What you cannot do is avoid giving feedback to your employ-ees. By withholding feedback, you deprive your employees of your contributions to their development and success. If the only time you talk to them about their career goals and performance is dur-ing an annual review, you're missing hundreds of opportunities to maximize strengths and improve performance. If you remain silent while subordinates make errors, or when they achieve goals, you do them, yourself, and your organization a tremendous disservice.

This guidebook has provided a simple but effective blue-print for building and managing a feedback relationship with your subordinates. The ability to provide feedback to subordinates is a skill that, with practice, you can carry out with confidence and with great effectiveness.

Subordinate Feedback Checklist

Consult this checklist regularly to remind you of the main elements involved when you give feedback to subordinates.

❑ Give feedback frequently.

❑ Make feedback timely. Don't wait too long after observing a subordinate's behavior.

❑ Keep feedback simple.

❑ Provide a private, neutral setting when your feedback concerns behavior that must be corrected.

❑ Focus on the situation you have observed.

❑ Describe the subordinate's behavior without interpreting motives.

❑ Communicate the impact of the subordinate's behavior.

❑ Offer your subordinates suggestions and support for making changes in their behavior.

❑ Take your subordinate's information style into account and be prepared for unexpected information.

❑ Leverage your subordinate's strengths.

❑ Catch people "doing things right."

Suggested Resources

Berke, D., Kossler, M. E., & Wakefield, M. (2008). *Developing leadership talent.* San Francisco, CA: Pfeiffer.

Fleenor, J. W., & Prince, J. M. (1997). *Using 360-degree feedback in organizations: An annotated bibliography.* Greensboro, NC: Center for Creative Leadership.

McCauley, C. D. (2006). *Developmental assignments: Creating learning experiences without changing jobs.* Greensboro, NC: Center for Creative Leadership.

McCauley, C. D., Ruderman, M. N., & Van Velsor, E. (Eds.). (2010). *The Center for Creative Leadership handbook of leadership development* (3rd ed.). San Francisco, CA: Jossey-Bass.

Roush, P. E. (1992). The Myers-Briggs Type Indicator, subordinate feedback, and perceptions of leadership effectiveness. In K. E. Clark, M. B. Clark, & D. P. Campbell (Eds.), *Impact of leadership* (pp. 529–544). Greensboro, NC: Center for Creative Leadership.

Van Velsor, E., Leslie, J. B., & Fleenor, J. W. (1997). *Choosing 360: A guide to evaluating multi-rater feedback instruments for management development.* Greensboro, NC: Center for Creative Leadership.

Background

The advice given in this guidebook is backed by CCL's research and educational experience, which has over the years demonstrated the value of (1) assessment for development and (2) systemic development.

Assessment for development has been a focus of CCL since its beginning in 1970. That year Robert Dorn, Ph.D., was named director of the Leadership Development Program (LDP)®. He had come from the Peace Corps, which practiced assessment for selection, where trainees were evaluated to determine whether they should receive assignments but were never told what was learned about them.

This was also the long-standing practice of the business world at that time, as reflected in the use of assessment centers to identify potential managers—the first such operational center having been set up by Michigan Bell in 1958.

Dorn had a different idea; he believed that if you tell people how they are doing, this information can help them do better. This simple but powerful notion was built into LDP, which, of course, is a feedback-intensive experience.

It was also understood from the beginning that developing the capacity to lead was not something that could be accomplished by a single, time-limited event. LDP was originally several weeks in length—before practicality dictated that it be condensed into one week. This understanding, shaped by CCL research on how executives learn from experience, and by the effort to follow up with participants of LDP and other CCL programs, has evolved into the recognition that leadership must be developed by means of a continual and systemic process, and that an essential aspect of this process is ongoing feedback.

A thorough explanation of these themes can be found in *The Center for Creative Leadership Handbook of Leadership Development* (Jossey-Bass, 1998), and in such CCL reports as *How to Design an Effective System for Developing Managers and Executives* (1996).

Key Point Summary

Given its potential to bolster improved performance, managers should eagerly supply feedback to their subordinates. But it doesn't happen often. Most people work without the benefits of effective feedback. For whatever reason, managers find it hard to give feedback to their direct reports. To succeed in your leadership role, you must learn how to make feedback a part of developing your direct reports to their full potential. More than that, you must learn how to provide effective feedback that is empowering, not damaging; that is constructive, not debilitating.

Giving feedback often gives you the best chance of reinforcing positive behavior and of influencing change in unacceptable behavior. You should also give feedback in a timely manner, and not wait too long to comment on a direct report's behavior. Making employees aware of potential opportunities and providing constructive steps they can take to achieve those goals are key motivations for providing effective feedback to subordinates. Addressing a performance problem is also a good use of feedback.

When giving feedback to your direct reports, be specific, keep it simple, and steer clear of interpreting behavior. It helps if you can catch direct reports doing things right, so that all your feedback isn't focused on negative behavior.

Giving feedback can provoke an emotional reaction. In dealing with feedback's emotional impact, take into account the individual situation; recognize that people process information differently; factor in health, personal, and family problems; and draw on your direct report's problem-solving abilities.

Like the other leadership skills you have developed, giving feedback to subordinates may at first feel unnatural and uncomfortable. Don't be concerned if your initial attempts are awkward. Take that first step. The ability to provide feedback to direct reports is a skill that, with practice, you can carry out with confidence and with great effectiveness.

Ordering Information

TO GET MORE INFORMATION, TO ORDER OTHER IDEAS INTO ACTION GUIDEBOOKS, OR TO FIND OUT ABOUT BULK-ORDER DISCOUNTS, PLEASE CONTACT US BY PHONE AT 336-545-2810 OR VISIT OUR ONLINE BOOKSTORE AT WWW.CCL. ORG/GUIDEBOOKS.